AMERICAN SCAPEGOAT

AMERICAN
SCAPEGOAT

Enzo Silon Surin

www.blacklawrence.com

Executive Editor: Diane Goettel
Book Design: Amy Freels
Cover Design: Zoe Norvell
Cover Art: Vincent Valdez
  Requiem
  graphite/paper
  2013
  Courtesy of the artist
  Photo credit: Peter Molick

Published 2023 by Black Lawrence Press.
Printed in the United States.

for Nicholas and Michael
&
for my tribe

Contents

American Scapegoat   3

I.
American asteRISKS (The George Floyd Suite)   7
Voyager   11
aperture   13
American Ethos (A Private War)   14
American Ethos (The South Bronx '98)   15
American Pathos   16
American Myth   17
Whether (An American Libretto)   19

II.
Gray's Anatomy (The Freddie Gray Suite)   27
American Ethos (Reacher Men)   33
In Defense of My Body's Dissertation   35
When Night Fills with Premature Exits   38
Prelude (weather is inevitable)   39

III.
In the Country of Chagrins and Mortuaries   43
American-ache   44
American Betr   a   y   a   l   l   47
American Testimony   51
some of us keep on dying   52

American Sermon (Elegy for Breonna Taylor)   53

American Ally   56

Prelude (some of us just keep dying)   57

IV.

Prelude (liberation is once and no more)   61

American Reprieve (A Here and Not-Here Division)   62

Elegy for the American Dream   72

V.

How to Craft an American Scapegoat   75

Interrogating Films About the End of the World   76

Interrogating Past & Future Constellations   77

American Miscellany   79

When My White Neighbor Offers Hope & A Garden Hose

    81

The Block Before Columbus   82

American Testimony (A Reprise)   84

American Pathos (What It Means to Love)   85

American Ethos (A Father's Admonition)   86

Prelude (in the beginning was the word)   87

VI.

Postlude (How to Make American
        History Grate Again)   91

American Lexicon (A Taxonomy of Pride)   92

Interlude (How to Build an American Legacy)   93

American Libretto (A Letter of Resignation)   94

Prelude (rhite wegrets: an american saga)   111

VII.

When History Returns as a Four Hundred-Year-Old
      Scapegoat   115
American Emblem (The Saga of a Black Avenger)   117
American Witness   119

Notes   121
Acknowledgments   123

The story begins with a tale
about atonement, and a promise,
and a goat, and a tribe favored by God

American Scapegoat

*

It started with a rouse: a yes meant death
a no meant death of a different kind

one yes meant a death we're familiar with
another meant possibility of only dying once.

*

Once we promised we would be willing
to trill, they wanted more, wanted loyalty

wanted more than lock-stock-barrel devotion
they wanted ancestral-cessation allegiance.

*

Cessation by word is not cessation
by heart, some say, so we said yes

but guns were never a way for us
to make *way out of no way*, a way.

*

As a way of making an example of us,
a harsh and public afterlife awaited—

every single day derided of our dignity
for refusing to take an oath that breaks an oath.

I.

"I'm the main character, played grandiose
Between two choric songs of tragedy,
And broadcast live…"
~ Erica Dawson

American asteRISKS (The George Floyd Suite)

*

by definition, a high
pitched voice is a falsetto
when it comes, "unnaturally,"
out the mouth of a dying man.

but this does not occur when
one is unable to breathe
naturally—by definition it is
done with intent—the man

and his neck and lungs must
be allowed to cycle breaths
freely. Otherwise, by definition,
it is called suffocation.

& when the only thing he is
resisting is death, a counterfeit
note is a need & a knee is simply
proof and not a new revelation.

*

the rope's decisively taut &
it never tires, wheeling in

all who cared to admire
the raiding & raising

up of black humans—
in trees, leaving nothing

to the imagination.
There was no mistaking

death was not the goal.
White humans, posing

next to the ornamented
remains meant hoisting

up a body was a far more
joyful way to shed one's sins.

*

if only a man could spit out his past
without blood trilling

from his mouth—American blood
spilling from within

from another man's manuscript
of a pastoral gasp & flooding

from where the moon hit
but didn't last & a keeling

year began on the same day
that man kept on swallowing

because he was taught like
we were taught, to hold it all in:

the past, the present & future
killings—all in one kneeling.

*

a knee bend means supplication
means utter submission in prayer
& rested assurance that gravity is
no match for the body's will to be

upright. it means one is willing to
collect what was once withheld as
promissory—a flag's omission of
a black obit black obit & perigee.

a knee band is a sign of rest and
respect, as in *bring it all in*, as in
a break from a history of breaks &
to *listen to the sound of my fleeting*

breaths in a circle of others fleeting.
Kaepernick took a knee in the quiet
& calm of his heart. what transpired
was a nation's hum of *move on* and

get gone. he took a knee for too many
obits in a Bluecoat Galaxy & called out:
we ain't the problem. He proved a knee
bend, by definition, is a premonition.

*

Rumor has it we lose an ounce
and a half of breath each day. But
if you are black, like me, and were born
mourning your rotations around the sun,
you're a full breath closer to the grave.
Why wasn't I born a person to you?
I bare the bane mask of alterations
from gravel across my face.
It's hard for the throat not to flit the past,
or the eyes not to roll back
far enough to glean the gathering
of huge crowds & camera flash. This is historic
in the sense it's been done before, when
blood ellipses covered the eyes
so discreetly there is no Coroner. *Holy*
is a shame we have no words for.
And future ellipses such as this:
a man will cry for his dead mother
as they draw closer to one another. That means
he'll bear witness to his own suffocation…
But these aren't just facts.
What harbors most is that one day
a white rope was left to corral around my neck
until every last breath is tried. Don't tell me
you don't see it. Everybody knows love
when they see it.

Voyager

You are a speck
azure & dust
in a galaxy
called potential

potential to bust
in that what have
you done for me
lately milky way

weight of the wait
says stop caring
before the world
does—in that you

are not going to
amount to anything
worth remembering
like a rogue planet

immigrant & black
second born, brother
of your father's son, a
speck through the lens

of ephemeral gazes &
constant stares—you
master constellations
like mazes—their eyes

heralding blue planets
& others filled with
oceans—in awe
of the possibilities—

galaxies light years
away—while at home
cities become oceans &
black moons become dust

& every day something
threatens to launch you
into the interstellar space
of your very own body.

aperture

after Lucille Clifton

accused of flunking a test
as if I took it,
as if I studied day
and night and bombed it. I did not:
results were waiting for me
when I came
bustling out of my mother's womb,
her *pride and joy,*
whose pigment, she feared,
there on her breast,
would habitually
test hope's resilience. I am
regaining memory every day,
cataloging names, dates
and places I was never supposed to
travel to on my own, without risking rope,
branch and a gullet full of bullets.

American Ethos (A Private War)

a cross, a black torso,
Someone's steady draw
of a decant clip.

turns out there's much left to fear.
the moon knows this reek.
Someone keeps writing

and writing and writing.
Someone you trust &
call "father" or call "brother"

delivers a gasp in contusions—
block's commotion bids for proof
of wrong doing—   & we blue,

not just blue-collared.
these rounds mean
            we don't matter—

not like Bluecoats
            navigating the same streets,
on their way home—   we, too

American Ethos (The South Bronx '98)

And daily, too, it seemed more plain
that this was no ordinary matter
—W.E.B. Du Bois

Forty-one shots is mean business. And fourteen
days before my twenty-second birthday, it meant
an accent was still a liability. Take Amadou Diallo.

By day, he sold videotapes, gloves and socks
on the sidewalks along 14th Street. One night
his silhouetted wallet, a dour and lowly black

square, bid as proof his name did not belong
in the fallible mouth of a 226's threaded barrel.
With an errant air, they demanded to see *papers.*

He made what was a natural choice & complied.
He did not know that would lead to his body's
last inscription. In New York City, these were

all too frequent lapses—all at a moment's notice
a stairway, a parking or corner lot was filled with
a severe light, short and sharp, like thundering rain.

& that night, another name was tossed into the hush
of an omen: a deliberate wallet could never make up
the difference spawned by a detective's clumsy feet.

American Pathos

they did not ask who he was
when he boarded that train

everything about him did not say
straight A student, momma's boy,

bully vic, sci-fi fanatic or after-school
guardian of a pig-tailed-baby-sister galaxy

in one svelte motion he entered a terrain
trying to board that train:

>   the glimmer of his belt buckle
>   the angle of his hands in his pocket
>   the hide and seek banter of a pack
>   of now-n-laters from baby sis

they did not say who they were
did not flash badges

he fit the description
so yields the inscription

>   *embed, embed a name*
>   *on that south bound train*
>
>   *embed, embed another name*
>   *on that south bound train.*

American Myth

I.

In America, reports on
boogeymen are manual.
They are fashioned

to deliberately shame
and maim. In them black
people become beasts,

the foul things of night-
mares, barbarians in need
of lashing, marauders

to be always kept
in the glare of pistols—
even a seventeen-year-old

with a hood & deliberate smile,
claiming *there was so much joy
in the boy, he must've stolen it.*

II.

There were riots. There were
lawsuits. There were bodies
and attempts to allay black fear.

There were exhibitions of force.
There were grand juries & more
dissertations about young & black

bodies being struck with a vertigo.
We insisted not all lives mattered.
But there were jabs. & more bodies.

& half a decade appears to be enough
time to not be able to distinguish
an omission from erasure: in three

out of three major search engines,
Ferguson by name refers to plumbing
and no mention of *Brown* or *Wilson*

or the *Oath Keepers* trolling on rooftops
or the suburb where there was so much
venom in a boy he had to be exorcized.

Whether (An American Libretto)

whether or not you believe in weather it will happen
to you, will find you without warning it doesn't care

whether or not it hurts is of no consequence nor a building's or levee's
collapse, or the trees the wind and nature's fury—a mother country
with no deal to be made and with no care about

whether or not you have been under the weight
of an already murderous reign and that your life regiment is regimes,
doesn't matter

whether or not despots have already marked these spots with death
the earth rumbled and crumpled huts and monuments alike, like it
didn't matter

whether or not we made a living out of the sum of dirt underneath our
fingernails or that it paled in comparison to the flamboyant trees'
retreat out of our reach or

whether or not we were heard, or that our history was misread or that
we believed despite being misled or that we were

the orphans of a republic that is
                    both bullet and barrel—
splitting our carapace like a cell splits
the body into hemo-spheres
                    both air and trumpet
splitting our cords into a memo—
read like an omen—splitting our chords
into particles and articles of refuse

we mattered like groans matter in a slum,
like leathery skin in the summer sun or like the sum
of a skillful gun that knows, whether we moan
or not, our absences will never trump
the lower breath snuffing us out

doesn't matter whether we quit these lipped hours
and the perpetual sweat

or that we quit that dumb other that prowls
that winter that mellows our minds
without hesitation,
the adage that *keepin' it real* is
dicing our breath on a defiant air
courting wreckage and it's worth it,

doesn't matter whether we quit that dumb other
without deliberation,
the benches peeled with by-gone bullets under
the direst of flight, or

the syphilitic revolvers that render the block cold as mines,
whether we pay our respects in the thug air of a mean retreat,
bereft of days,
bereft of nights,
when we quit that dumb other that says
              some are born to smile

              doesn't matter
whether we quit the trap that rendered us neutral,
noise which crows all correction is connection,

the obligatory dictation in our mouths exalting us
for our tribe-lingual amputations,

that pillaged choice,
that Pat Booned our voice,

whether or not we quit noise which gleams all things correctional
as correction,
that thing which causes us to hone moan
as anthem—groan so long we mime life,
back-slash black, this what-we-did-before
hypomnesia, memory gone so long we hone groan, or

whether or not we quit that unmistakably labored tone
the umbilical hazing of our sanctuaries—

or whether many of us drew dirt prematurely—our genealogy
of deficit that begat deficit that begat too many
names we will never learn to know by heart,

doesn't matter
whether we're still standing
                    and free

our mouths deciphering
the saline
of tears from all
other salty liquids

the masters of our own
hope and despair—

inciting
reciting
a hello grin
as we wade
in the science
of goodbye

to pry
that exilic snowflake
from the barrel of our throat

we wake we wake we wake we wake

it never mattered whether or not our dreams were real, or were abated
or if the wait alone was worth its weight in being elated, it didn't
matter

whether or not that these spots on these blocks used to take a backseat
to the heat with beatboxing and slap boxing for fun, when it didn't
matter

whether or not we wore our Kangols backwards or if a fitted cap from
the hatter didn't truly mean or result in a new era, we didn't care

whether its leathery skin kicking game in pleather or a wool sweater—
the cold's often colder for those having problems keeping their shit
together—it didn't matter

whether we knew better than to let pockets full of cream trump the
thought of being ashy we were always a check we prayed the streets
would never cash and it didn't matter

whether our toes braved below-frozen and in a gnome pose or the
corner was an epistle or however the streetlights came up was how we
were going to be remembered, didn't matter

whether or not we mouthed the gully sidewalk or how some of us
never drew more than lint from their pockets and still tasted
pavement, it didn't matter

whether or not they made a living dubbing us the sum of dirt
underneath fingernails or that nothing paled in comparison to their
flamboyant piece's retreat out of our reach

we've always known we mattered like heartbeats in a drub, like the
sum of a skillful gun
that knows, whether we hone moans, groans, our absences will never
trump the lower breath
snuffing us out.

II.

...a bleat is heard
from the vacuum of erasure

Gray's Anatomy (The Freddie Gray Suite)

I

Imagine a tin can's semi-erratic clang
as it is transported—without restraint
—in the back of an empty, lauded truck.

Imagine a rag doll or the fling of a mop's flop
or a rogue, freshly peeled honeydew melon
at the mercy of the groove-floor-bed of a truck.

Imagine a shell-less soft-boiled egg or a baked
sweet potato rolling off the makeshift counter
of a bench. Imagine it being tossed in the truck

like it is born of a dung-sack nation. Imagine it
has ears and can ear itself crack open. Imagine
you can hear it crack open in the back of a truck

and it sounds like a tea kettle whistle. Imagine it
is the sound the throat makes when it has broken
away from its voice box. Imagine a man attached

to the voice and the throat and the sound of a cry
that sounds like something has cracked open and
imagine he tosses haplessly in that metal truck and

nobody gives a fuck—not the driver of the truck—
how the man's body failed to flutter to the ground
as he lost consciousness, how the clanging of cuffs

were one of the last sounds he heard, & how his gut
may have felt when he entered the back of that truck
he was on the verge of being relegated to compost.

II

depraved-heart murder is sixth,
alphabetically, under the terms
for *homicide* in U.S. criminal law—

comes right before *execution-style
murder*, which, by definition, is
when one is killed at close range,

which is to say in close proximity
& *under complete physical control
of an assailant* & who has been left

with no chance *of resistance or escape*.
This is to say when they clicked their
own seatbelts in, they knew the law—

knew the risk of death or injury & kept
on driving. They knew the law because
they were the law. That itself was clear.

But this was Baltimore & be more was
not just a dub but an omen for the truth,
as in it could not be any more apparent

that being black means you have signed
a poor lease & Bluecoats know all about
laws & the savor of just how to break 'em.

III

report has it a bolt left an impression on your head.
it's how they determined your life was not secured

properly. there was no harness or safety net. you left
behind a twin sister. she might have felt what you felt.

that's not even close to the beginning of how we've
dealt—same headlines & proverbial bob-n-weave:

he resisted arrest by jabbing the air with his head—must
have been how it happened—necks keep breaking *trust*

falls of those who *serve and protect.* what we have been
saying is a man whose daily rations is time spent kneeling

is not a zealot but a man in the unrelenting custody of one
out to drub a city of black faces into the *most woebegone.*

and we let them. city snaps a neck and writes a check &
we let them. no one's held responsible for your death &

IV

radical revolution begins with
a revelation: the end of values
& to the number of times one
forces the mind & tries to rehab
hope as *alternate ending* to a life
being hauled, cuffed in the back
of a van so the hands could not
brace fall or bulrush of swerves.

because we don't lose the same,
he was left to a hush of nerves—
premature ending—& three fractured
vertebrae & a crushed voice box.
no matter who consented or whose
myths about breeds dubs black men
fugitives, whose news makes one altar
an epistle and another grave or whose
blues lines the street *too often*, radical
rotations begin with loss, which means
being *woke* is never the same as being
a wake in one's own body.

& because we don't lose the same
amount of sleep—not over three
fractured vertebrae or a crushed
voice box, it is all a *tragic end* &

one does not need eyes to see this:
place a hand on the page & you can
make out the breaking of his voice—
it is like the clearing of your throat.

American Ethos (Reacher Men)

No human being can
deny the kowtow
scene in a backyard

where a man appears
to be praying among
blades of grass—striking

his face again, and again
—look closely and he is
rinsing his face in a pool

of his own blood. Look
closer and he is wearing
handcuffs to keep his hands

from worship, his arms are
braced against his back—not
armed & ominous as they will

claim. Listen, he is trying to say
reach for breath—call misplaced
on the phone. Who will speak now

for him? The body's enough evidence
but boys-in-blue drub within the rules
and never offer supplication for being

in the wrong yard & say death was
gloating *either them or me*—& that
somehow makes them in the right—

and that seems enough for most—
same ones who were told Pluto's no
longer a planet & believed that shit.

In Defense of My Body's Dissertation

I

The distance between all bodies of matter
in the solar system is an Astronomical Unit,
or AU, which means all dark space in Space
is measured in spans too immense to grasp—

yet light travels within such spaces—it takes
499.0 seconds for light to travel from the sun
to Earth—one Astronomical Unit—for light
to travel between two distances and be seen—

which means the distance between a hand and
a gun is measured by how fast light travels
between two human beings orbiting the same
block—on the one hand, this means there isn't

a way to tell the difference between a known
or rogue planet wandering the cosmos without
stars—to make suspect out of them or gun out
of wallet, an asteroid to be blasted from the sky.

II

Look,
I'm not saying
I know how
the body knows
when
it is being
sized up
for plunder—
braving the shelling
of smuggled smug
smiles
everyday and still
find a way to
squeeze into
a slightly snug pair
of sweatpants & t-shirt
at day's end, to trick
the skin into comfort,
when all it wants
to do is recount
the head lines
one by
one, & the bygones:
slug,
slug,
slug

III

& because you don't believe me when I say
I think the air is trying too hard not to fill
my lungs. Because it should be easy. It should
be easier. To breathe. But I wear atmosphere
like a blue skin. And learn to become familiar
with the word *strata*. It means: a region
of atmosphere; a layer of tissue deep
stratum of the skin; a layer in which
archaeological material (such as artifacts,
skeletons, and dwelling remains) is found
on excavation; a part of a historical or socio-
logical series—a period of development; a
socioeconomic level of society—especially
regarding education or culture; a statistical
subpopulation. I'm convinced. I am the miles
between the moon and here. Dark. Still. Matter.

When Night Fills with Premature Exits

Is there a place where black men can go
to be beautiful? Is there light there? Touch?

Is there comfort or room to raise their black
sons as anything other than a future asterisk,

at risk to be asteroid or rogue planet but not
comet—to be studded with awe and clamor

and admired for radial trajectories across
a dark sky made of asphalt and moonshine

to be celebs and deemed *a magnificent sight?*

Prelude (weather is inevitable)

Winters here are so cold even
the trees are in permanent bow.

In spring & summer the branches
tickle the top of our heads in banter

as if in the months prior they did not
threaten to sever eyes from our heads.

We live among their shade too.
We have no choice. We know there is

something here much worse than trees.
& the birds know it too.

III.

"Pressed to the wall, dying, but fighting back!"
~ Claude McKay

In the Country of Chagrins and Mortuaries

Every day I wake up & get dressed for my own funeral
and glance at the dead man arrayed in the mirror like
a clock, & the distance between rooms tries to reconcile
the news, & tying my shoes with a pair of trigger fingers
feels like *this is it*—what an omen would yield if it were
a member of the body & this body is not as beautiful as
the bodies from where you're from, because this body
isn't *beautifully bodied* where you're from, though this
body is more beauty embodied where I am from—and
being best dressed in a pleasant smile does not mean
I won't meet the worst of the world's finest assassins
& it won't mean a prowl car isn't rehearsal for a hearse
& it won't mean I will know what to make of screaming
white boys in cars and their bodies bungling in and out
of bars & who often tell police to fuckoff & live, & brag
—& habitually wake solely in the custody of a hangover.

American-ache

-ade

1

we cling to lemons
for clearing

we cannot tell
zipper from mouth

an ardent sting
enamel strippers

motive hater of palates

lemons always know
how to reach you

2

pants seams pry
open, a glare

nailing posts - affirm
graviton theory

birds can't help
dead their poses

blocks kelp don't
dead their Moses

lemons always know
how to reach you.

3

block disinfectants
sip c-note juice sideways

bike wheels scale
a broken torso

eye-young a crowd
creased between crisp

cracks, a new brand
lemons always know

lemons always know

how to reach you.

-ache

wake   in any language
set the timer   to breach,
brush your animal   clean

make this map
from dividends.   *say it!*
how long it will take

to number these frames,
& phrases   to make your mean
a means for being

along the wrong terrace,   always
& later   among the shards
casings upon casings

& traces
traces
traces.

American Betr a y   a l l

Unimaginative
        ears
                here

                                                        stray,

        Cumber,
subscription to
                mellow
                                These streets
                                come night-
                fall's not
                More bars,   more
windows
        but doors.
Appease to
        pastoral chorus
                        of   no,
                              go,
                              slow
Assemble
        migration,   for myopic

                symbolic   climb,
dissent
                betrayal of light,
        day's
                        dulled out

                reflection
                                of blades and

breath is like a perchance of

what comes naturally to the senses—
making naturally   what comes to neighbor
hood's heap of jabbers   and mourners
concentration of bones, of lovers
leaving   diversions
of those left between

summer yields it gleams
traffic lights   hydrant arches stream cold
                                 heat's incapacitated
ritual   what comes naturally
to the make
shift sensors   we call
love what we call   factions
                                 of fractions of love
the decadent equation
                        multiplied by   one   shot
two
shots three shots   four
one block   new block

                                    mira, pour

*

we soldier on down
horrendous streets—
we don't know which

way to walk,
all around us,
a fresh white

breaks open in a tenement.
Squared suddenly into
ditches—we accumulate

dust from
hovering ash, skin.
Seems we were just

mixing stars for passersby
and blankets & for
a moment we thought

> could treble
> the sand with songs
> of mortals and potters.

We weighed letters
from home on our tongues
before they varied.

Now a few more
uses for a mouth—
One: an infinite appeal

for the torso's skeletal opus.
Two: a bed for the voice's
feigned coma.

Three: a throated clod
of dirt, to be forgotten.
We don't know which

way to draw back,
waking up swiftly
in a head-to-toe world

where everything is
white. A renovated air
bulges with sand.

We spurt in any direction.
We don't know which way
to war. The only visible road

offers no access.
So many open mouths
between us, so much
crimson

breaking
from
marrow.

American Testimony

i wish i could write about bees and collapsed colonies &
about a young child frolicking through fields of withered
posies in search of something whole and tender, with their
head down & crying about the promise of all that is unseen.

i wish this could be a verse about extinction and preventing
lions & other wildcats from meeting the fate of a rifle's aim
& about how a broken tooth will always remind us of Cecil,
whose murder caused a nation to hold its head down and cry.

i wish i were writing about a beached whale or a pack of sea
lions who mistook the sand for stardust or heavenly grounds
& how a village of strangers nursed & ushered them back to
the sea—watching, arm-on-shoulder, & heads down, crying.

i wish what is written was about a rare moth that once made
a dilapidated shack its home, and how it was spared minutes
before demolition, & how it was the man who built the shack
that discovered it, and how he held his head down and cried.

instead i am writing in hope that you will care about my early
demise, enough to be moved by how often i find myself on my
knees & wailing under a dilapidated sun and how your head is
often constantly held down so you don't ever have to see me die.

some of us keep on dying

and we are talking about a kill-shot, not
fake bruises or a feline musing on a fake-
tailed mouse, and a real house filled with
windows wide enough to see through and
no shades or barricade, just lemonade—not
on a stand but in the veins from being ones
interrogated ad nauseam & without charges.

understand: there's no way of knowing how
sweet from that distance, you say, and must
be close enough to be a cup or a mouth or a
cop musing as both and so you tell yourself
if only I were a cup or cop and in that room,
if only I were able to take a sip, to know for
sure how one winds up killed-dead in custody.

American Sermon (Elegy for Breonna Taylor)

every person on their knees
ain't praying & every ending
to a prayer is a lie about
in whose name one offers
supplication—if any at all.

we know this because
repentance comes in
the form of sin. It is a lie
about keeping a promise
about a promise: *to protect*
& serve—it is a lie
about a lie.

we know this because
she was killed in her own
home. & it was legal.

we know this because
"you may die" is the anthem
of no-knocks or low-knocks
at a front door & a warrant
without warrants. & it was
all legal.

& whether you believe in
miss takes or in lies or in
the quagmire of "justice"
vs "just us", when she was
killed, she was not breaking
the law. the bluecoats did.
but it's legal. we know this
because no charges were
filed & she is still dead.

they called 911 because
they were scared. it didn't
matter. she was an EMT.
it didn't matter. they were
the police. we know which
truth was true. all the casings
they dropped. & no charges
filed?

we've been saying lemons
always know how to reach
us. we keep being told to
make lemonade when life
brings us zingers. & we
keep saying it is still legal
to mirandize us with a bullet.

& still the light keeps
passing on over us.
it seems there aren't
enough amens and
hallelujahs to save us.

& maybe you will have to
lose as much to understand.

it has never been the rule of
law to pry your tears in a gullet
full of bullets.

& we've always been
who the law was always
meant to protect you from.

American Ally

At some point I am going to die
and you will have played a role
in my death—having contributed
nothing to cease the deceasing—

with your rank & file *we are all
the same* & that bleary conceit to
not see color but know precisely
the number of friends you have

that are non-white & the number
of arrests they don't have because
they are *one of the good ones* and
they are *not like the rest of them.*

Your conscience is the keeling kind.
You may not see *color* but know how
to separate light from dark, & divide
the cosmos aptly in your own image.

Tell me, how did I become *asteroid*
& you *comet*? How does one Prophet
& the other profits? Tell me, what is
a doppelgänger? & what is legacy?

Prelude (some of us just keep dying)

Sometimes there is nothing you can do.
A failed State is an unkept promise. It is
glue at the bottom of your shoes on *way
to the airport*. It is an arrow in your back
on way to the sea. It is a rotten grenade
on the road that leads to the only road left
out of town. Which means somebody must
throw their body on it if the rest of us are to
make it out. Which is to say, it might mean
having to throw your own body on it if you
are to make it out alive.

IV.

This is when it's good to know
a group of goats is called a tribe.

Prelude (liberation is once and no more)

to you,
dead voice
from me, a living one

I do not write these
words
thinking that

you will head them.
I know your heart has
braved much: buried in

the osmious valence
of a new stack
of bones.

American Reprieve (A Here and Not-Here Division)

After Rita Dove

Among us: blazed ones, cold bricks,
corner gnomes—cirrhotic livers—in
fragmented lush, dreams a melancholy
hue—fists for fights and dents—winter,
a breath season. Remnants of monster
days—a collar's hemmed up contra-
diction, a noose: soot, burn stains, proud
tenants show-and-prove worthy of scars.
Wander these rock-filled parking lots,
smiles spackled with grief tilt up
before blanking in repair—walk past
their elongated gaze. Beneath blue tracks,
train veins fill with a torched heaven. No,
we won't cry—for this could speak no year.

~

We won't cry for this—could. Speak? No. Years
we've longed for brief withdrawal—'hood
closure—a fought living, a colossal chant.
The air's too tamed to trust flight. Mainly
we can't imagine what's beyond it. Mainly
we've sought comfort in the wrong corners.
Morning no longer leads a full wake—day
rolls over, slants slow, sleeps most—a
solemn hum accounts for the stirring, ones
who spend most nights waiting, cramped
within dimmed-down hallways—deftly
prod for future 'hoods—precisely a rustic
song: *I wonder if heaven got a ghetto* and
how much longer must we stay here?

~

How much longer—must we stay here?
Time comes as pistols, as man-made
holdups. What we've done for the way
out: at the base of the bridge, summer
ball court, a fertile soil—call it hope—
dribbling Jordan heirs, unison sprints
—in a wrist's flash the ball ascends
a spin so perfect with no desire to break.
Eternity standing on the side for next.
Come hard or come prepped to sway
with your gear. Look, he's got the new
King James'—ground's air under them.
How much for their selling these days
brother? Momentum losing—again.

~

Brother, momentum's losing—again.
Winter's pier makes bitter men.
Neighborhood discretion sparks
dampness—run, chew park fences
—bus stops bawl—breeds territorial
counter-movement, muffs the peace—
young clans of bedlam—'hood despair
at primo—blocks collect every hit—
lively chatter straps the corner—share
isn't a weight in limit. It sure don't work
none to complain. Charge white folks?
A kept sum: fronting a kinship yields
a better ace. Crack's luster days recant—
eyes selecting what want we govern. Obit.

~

Eyes selecting what we want govern? Obit:
no curative for the ailment of thug-life—
perennial spastic silhouettes hover the city.
Will the streets ever have their fill of this
tasteless, inexhaustible wine? Purpose
our young girls, we're failing—they inure
with flips of eyelids—a throng of men woo,
proffer warmth—promises of *blowing
backs out* brings valor—a true wonder?
No one's seen one. Aftermath: desolation—
morning, a dubious sequel—what we inherit?
A prelude, a blues to fill the mouth—its rustic
taste, acquired. Paid in full's enmity's tag.
Held self hostage so long, we're now prolific.

~

Held self-hostage so long we're now prolific.
Barrel and crab lexicon: *nigga;* a pocket
exchange—words and shells, street camps
cold—luring with pre-tension, a reckless
provoking when in passing, head nod in greet
now symbol for mistrust—what we've done
is mate it cool when white kids can brand
the ether with *nigga*—can't heel this pace for-
ever. Who will guide-back the bailouts, back
into homes—humdrum words just won't do—
all too familiar with the danger of *what ifs*—
the indigent divide must soften its hold; and
making the difference—first steps: respite for
mother; father must stay home—all together.

~

Mothers, fathers must stay home altogether
if children are to garner discernment
rapt *beneath the shadow of a mighty*
grief, gushing over tennis shoes,
iced out crucifixes, wheel's chrome.
Lord, prime these children—will this breach
obsolete. They watch us praise, our voices
hoarse from exalting false Hope on the block,
not wanting to grieve the "we"—an irony:
our women carrying heartbreak to bed,
our men edging up sulking street corners,
their five o'clock shadowy faces echoing
once daring, self-assured warriors at peak—
men who were intact, now, remain in pieces.

~

Men who were intact now remain in pieces
—the scarred relics of a muddled past—
these monstrous broken men, the 'hood's
most celebrated (a sell-out tag awaits
the first to put himself together)—muscling
through mismanagement of wages, mostly
shifting weight—brazen in a grief, pendants
the size of Wonder bread slices—noosed
diamonds, be-mocking hope—this order
our new Babylon? Block's luster ensnares
even the boastful—what of the harvest,
all we've gathered as impetus for means,
glazed with an ever and anon travail when
Young Jesus's what we've dubbed dope dealer?

~

Young Jesus is what we've dubbed dope dealer.
We've also bemused our prophets for profit—
our bodies feeding on a fame-toxin that leaves
no trace of an outcast blood. It's a patented
labor, being hungry-poor—half-sown seeds,
topmost detained—no progress. Atonement line
spots some a lead—compensation-coalition for
even keel—but some *cop that, pimp that*—under
an electric hum, pant seats sag, weighted dream
—in souled-out venues, a familiar boast: *more*!
throw your hands in the air, like you don't care.
New frontier bursting at the seams—slug's
motivation: *now somebody, anybody, scream!*
Outside, butter-yellow moon—burnt-toast sky.

~

Moon, butter-yellow side out—burnt-toast sky
temps first to leave the stoop—albeit the rest,
stride unyielding—'til what we've trained for:
precision, speed, endurance—all that's keen
bolsters our legs to brave the pushed wind—
'til fathers reinstated, inurn this blues—flash
of rebirth—path a new *how*, unearth clout once
dormant; cast the dice in effigy, flasks no longer
mouthed, where plans lingered so long they turn
to moss—'til frequently: *no more sudden leaps*—
our women (hearts will calm)—*no pulling aces*
out of these *no-harm sins, &* we'll treble ground,
placing scamps on notice, pace the driven winters
among us: blazed ones, the cold bricks.

Elegy for the American Dream

When it reads "this could be you"
it doesn't mean you. You are not
the *they* or *them* of advertisements.

You are "the dead, arrayed in time"
of Pablo Neruda's *The Chosen Ones*
—the butt of jokes and machetes—

you are not a feature in these stories.
You are the withheld sneeze, you
are the closed-mouthed cough, &

a cupped yawn, you are hearsay—
the practical omission of first editions
and reports—not even byline in this

scene of bread and wine, an nsec—
not the target of ads that say "if you lived
here, you'd be home now." You are

a dog's yelp in the back of a truck, soon
to be fairytaled as the Hosanna of hyena
ghosts. You are, at best, a funereal hymn,

which means your body is a gravesite and
the city in which you orbit is a mass grave,
to which not everyone in this ad is invited.

V.

"If the embodiment of holiness,
if the embodiment of truth is White,
then someone like me can only hope
to be Holy, can only hope to be full of truth."
~ Christena Cleveland, PhD

How to Craft an American Scapegoat

make him a young boy in a project yard
make his pants sag like a deferred dream
make his momma not his real momma, his
daddy, ghost. fill his eyes & mouth with bias
so he resembles a child not like your child
but one blood-born and raised in a dung-sack
nation. make his hands rebel against the Union
by putting a pistol in his hands, christen him:
militant or desperado, someone who preys
on his neighbors, brothers, sisters and friends,
as a reaper who wants the chances that you
took. make him an aftermath or compilation
of fraught dead things. make his house one
created dangerously with memories & hearsay
about *huddled masses yearning to breathe free.*
poster him *the tired-poor*—a colossus of ails and
depredation. make him Lazarus. make him Black.

Interrogating Films About the End of the World

In movies it is always too late
when one finds out the world's
about to end—all the things
placed into it are suddenly like
coins in a meter in an empty lot.

Realizing it is not the end yet
but the beginning of the end
offers no solace because you
know it is coming and there is
nothing you can do about it.

And all the things placed into it
are now martyrs in that meter or
like bullets in the ether of a dark
parking lot, where a Bluecoat plays
God & you let him—are convinced

the world and all the things you have
placed into it are being taken from you.
Movies do that. And killing off black
characters, we know, is *in the script*:
loathe the looting and the looters, not

the fact the world is coming to an end
for all of us—riots & burnings fill up
the screens—certain that all you have
placed into the world or've yet to are
in danger, when we, too, are in danger.

Interrogating Past & Future Constellations

My oldest son asks
where stars come from
and I tell him what
I've been taught about
the stars being millions
or even billions of years old
since that's how much time
it takes for their light to reach
us down here on planet Earth.

Didn't have the heart to tell
him this also means the stars
might already be dust or gone
when they arrive in splendor
for us all to gaze and admire—
their metaphoric link to black
bodies riddled with holes that
shimmer and shine light years
from their primordial infliction.

We stand under an unlit street
lamp, calling out all the stars
that we can see, trying my best
to map out all the constellations.
His eyes are fast becoming
moons but the motion of his
five-year black body is what
concerns me—the years of his
childhood becoming extinct.

We are taught an object a light-
year away or more's being seen
as it was at the time light left it,
not as it would appear if one was
near it today. Somehow, we have
managed to make sense of a night
sky riddled with holes that shimmer
& shine. This is proof that we have
no qualms with admiring the dying.

American Miscellany

found

in a city & on a street you've never seen,
a little boy's blond hair's static cling is
briefly singed in an autumn afternoon sun

missing

in Bay St. Louis, Mississippi, a pigtailed
black little girl blows bubbles with *juicy*
glimmered on the butt of her sweatpants

scapegoat

at Coney Island, an empty stomach
rations a slice of bread into intervals
of three & foiled in a paltry landscape,

a thug lies on the sidewalk conjugating
karma—in an America of miscellaneous
oil spills and campaign promises

suffer(s)

metaphors for loss—the earth tosses
and turns, nocturnal shocks and waters
outwitting the flapping of hands—

judgment

we drift in and out in Orleans Parish—home
of the Bluetick Coonhound, shotgun shacks
where a pastor in earnest delivers a sermon

still, three hundred and sixty-five days to
a congregation of four—the rest remain
classified as missing—in The District, sky

floods with tightly spun basketballs—under
the bling of metal nets, a 26-year-old baller
ties his shoelaces beneath an epileptic sun.

witness

in miscellaneous america, home of hypomanic
chumps, a cardboard cut-out of Langston Hughes
as a busboy still contends for equal compensation

witness!

& children, malnourished, bank the river—no one
tells them it's not the Nile, it is manmade—it is a
battered woman, birthing dead fish from her womb.

When My White Neighbor Offers Hope & A Garden Hose

I should have known better than to say *yes*. But
with many years spent taking things out of kindness,
one's tongue is a prolific autopilot & purveyor of pleas
said softly and under one's breath like *help! please! Jesus!*
Which is to say when he offered it and a few other items
once he & his wife move, it was hard to say no. *We have
no use for them,* he says, & I nod the same bobble as when
he tells me that he couldn't believe the riots & how people
burning down stores had ruined things. He kept saying *they*.
I kept wondering if he meant looters. I mentioned the year
Boston was almost set on fire: the Red Sox broke the Curse.
He kept saying *they* & shaking his head about statues being
torn down & the Columbus losing its head on national TV.
I mentioned the nationally televised murder of Greg Floyd.
He offered a brief silence. He and his wife were sweet to us.
He kept shaking his head in disbelief at the beheading. *It is
not right,* he says. *There are other ways to make things better.*
He offered me a hose as a going away present. *We don't need it,*
he says. Tomorrow, my oldest will ask why the world's on fire.

The Block Before Columbus

The neighbors never called nine-one-
one on us. Not when I spent a summer
learning to ride a bike in the hallways
of our apartment building. Not when

a neighbor's door played goalpost and
we took turns launching penalty kicks.
Not when we threw water balloons off
the fire escapes in bombardment of rats

below—if we got too close to humans
they knew who our families were and
some had permission to scold & shame
us out of bedlam—Not then & not when

we littered the air of the front stoop with
laughter way past dusk, trying to expel
a summer heat that made a kiln out of
upper-floor apartments. Not one, ever. &

someone was always watching us. & when
the police stopped to interrogate our laughter,
flipping the lint out of our pockets & breaking
up what didn't need to be broken, the neighbors

vouched & pleaded. Some of us were still taken
for questioning, for good measure—the rest often
kept vigil in the lobby. & and on most nights, we
avoided the stoop altogether. & some pled & fled

& stopped laughing as loud & hung out less. Still
the police kept coming though no one called.

American Testimony (A Reprise)

i cannot run for Ahmaud Arbery.
i cannot run for Ahmaud Arbery.
i cannot run for Ahmaud Arbery.
i cannot run for Ahmaud Arbery.
i cannot run for Ahmaud Arbery.
i cannot run for Ahmaud Arbery.
i cannot run for Ahmaud Arbery.
i cannot run for Ahmaud Arbery.
i cannot run for Ahmaud Arbery.
i cannot run for Ahmaud Arbery.
i cannot run for Ahmaud Arbery.
my body becomes a city when I run.
and in American cities, black bodies
become mortuaries when they run.

American Pathos (What It Means to Love)

After Vievee Francis

There are more than several ways to love someone. You already know
most of them. I've watched you make love to a dog (so to speak)
by kissing it on its mouth so often it became a world.
And in that world people like me become *beast*. Not like a cherubim
but something dubbed the foulest creature, worthy of only
the foulest language that often comes with a foaming of the mouth
and a whiteness that parts the white firmament of your eyes
with a daub of redness. Is there only room for love in your world
saved for neighbor, and God and Country? Are you willing
to give up everything for what
you consider the highest form of Honor and Purpose? Which is to say
it is a form of godlessness when purity is only for white sheets
and deliberate creases. I know you know about what it means
to love—and to greet me with more than a faithless hiss
the next time we see each other on the street. Will you
meet me with more than grief and rifles? & tell me how
it feels to forget the heart is its own mirror, & what it means to love
the version of yourself that sermonizes me as: *profitable, foul & sullied*?

American Ethos (A Father's Admonition)

Do not lean on this world
for comfort, it is neither
shoulder nor shelter, and not
real in the way you imagine

or have been told—the way it is
presented in photographs from
outer space is far from the space
you occupy—not in your image or

borne of your imagination—and all
you have heard about choices and
being free to make them isn't meant
for you or those who look like you.

Earth is over 4.5 billion years old
but much of that's been claimed and
labeled for you. You choose but are
much too young to discern the void

in your choices. There's much to fill
you in on & timing is everything. Take
comfort in knowing that you matter—
though not in the way others seem to

matter. & by others, I mean white:
to be white is to be American; & to
be American is to be an Empire—
one nation, under God, indivisible.

Prelude (in the beginning was the word)

There are hidden
passages
in every faith—

some lead to
salvation
& others lead

to utmost ruin.
Both yearn for
a conclusion one is

prone to live with,
& one that one is
certain came from God.

VI.

If you protect the lie, you can save the village

Postlude (How to Make American History Grate Again)

.45

tell a boy he's a man and his penis
a pistol for shooting without permit,
ditto for killing black lives duty-free.
tell him "legacy of your forefathers"
not their obsession with foreskin and
brown skin or the red glare of rockets—
tell him an erection's *for an equation*
to be solved. say anything to make him
think it's *his duty,* how *a woman's body*
is no epistle so he'll consider it *a favor,*
he'll consider it *a bit of fun.* tell him his
pistol is an apostle for all-white glory,
glory hallelujahs, tell him he is praised
& worthy so he will start to believe his
~~erection~~ election's a reflection of us all.

American Lexicon (A Taxonomy of Pride)

to brag means to boast, as in to raise a flag made out of humans
    fleshed & hung,
as in to string a body up a flagpole, also called *tree*, at half mast—
    out of respect
for those who dote on the thoroughfare of a good shot or view of
    what democracy
looks like under a beautiful and spacious sky; to post a bill in honor
    of the *American Way*
for the return of those who braved being sold and torn by
    restless seas to harvest
endless amber waves of grain; to crown one's good as standard and
    fill the streets and halls
and chambers with cacophony 'bout *lost nation*, relics & fertile
    swamps gone feral;
to call into action nobler men to arouse the brotherhood of a shining
    sea undimmed
by human tears, and runback the years when heroes proved in
    liberating strife, a great and
whiter jubilee.

Interlude (How to Build an American Legacy)

turn your greatest desire into a memory
turn your greatest desire into a memory
turn your greatest desire into a memory
turn your greatest desire into a memory
turn your greatest desire into a memory
turn your greatest desire into a memory
turn your greatest desire into a memory
turn your greatest desire into a memory
turn your greatest desire into a memory
turn your greatest desire into a memory
turn your greatest desire into a memory
turn your greatest desire into a memory
tell a story about your greatest memory
& again, like it is your greatest memory

American Libretto (A Letter of Resignation)

at the brim of these lipped hours
silence
        split, like a spine splits the body into
        hemispheres; like when the carapace splits
        and cracks in two and every other split
        is a faction, a fraction of two—like
        when the blocks busted up in carnage
        split into two mothers burying sons—
        one traditionally, the other above ground
        —both eternally splitting a sum-grief
        divisible by two hands finger-split
        held and weaved like baskets,

        murder is a split-verb,
        splitting flats, flattening split-
        level townhouses into particles
        and articles of gray

why weren't we born to blanks?

the stack always sets to split:
splitting the face like cabbage
into mercurial, conjugal layers;
splitting the have-nots like lint
in a brokered pocket—hand's
always reaching, hand always
leeching on
deficit, always breeching the delicate
fate that splits in two truths:
        water can swallow
        or be swallowed—

splitting the face for cabbage,
splitting the macho
splitting the macho
splitting the macho
splitting the match *yo!*—split that
wrapper, that lid for liter—
the mouth gasping for a swig of hops—

whose night won't be split like air on a lipped trumpet?

who woke the world brown-lipped?
split and read like an omen:
con-fused, cons
fusing a split cell, split from level-headedness,
splitting and splitting as we grow into a memory,
as the spine grows into memoir and splits the body
into hemispheres into a memory,
into names we will never learn
to know by heart

at the brim of these lipped hours—
we dice with glances of unrequited love
          the way within forged
          with loaded fists
          in our pockets

to fight monsters we create monsters

is that gat that goes rat attack tact tack tact tact—

is the universe city of hunger
where *our skin is black from the heat of famine*

where the maybach treads a trend
upon the back of our memories

is the dimness when the sounds
we make are foreign: *home is not
my own*—moan so long we hone *gone*

is the epidermis the wind splits into
factions, fractions of blue

is that fusty anthem that says:
      some are born to smile
      and we reeve that
      like a pendant

      pockets full of cream
      but our thoughts, still ashy

why we weren't born to blanks—

is that muffled agony
      feeling like a check
      praying the streets
      will never cash

we wake we wake we wake—

park benches becoming a respite
for those who gurgle blood

and mornings bring
mourning to our marrow

he ain't our child
but they all our child

a whole day made of sulks
socks by the wayside, sobs
leading to graves

we wake we wake we wake—

at brim of these lipped hours
a mother rocks a picture frame
in her unpliable arms,
swaddling a dream:
a fatty plump of joy, whose bygone cackling
renders a primal scream
        for what
        for what was
        for what was once within her clench
        all that was once the making of a beautiful boy

he ain't our child
but they all our child

a loss is a loss is a loss is a—

the white lines will be stricken
from record,
street sweepers will pummel
particles of brown skin
down into cracks of tar
that the air will later refurbish

as pollen we inhale
        we inhale
        we inhale
        we inhale
        we in hell!
           gasping on sooty air
           that splits our lungs into Articles,
           particles of gray
living out our days
in the milk of sadness
stroking our way
to the block's circumferential
edge, ever so slowly
so as not to turn this pool of fears
into a slippery mess
so as not to cause more wakes

still
we wake we wake we wake we—

free but not carefree
learning how to make trenches
every
day

brooding over whose lid won't be split
like air on the lipped trumpet?

at the brim of these lipped hours
is the postscript
of the tongue's amputation,
the mouth's round the clock succession
and street epitaph:

an engine's muted *whirr* tapers
and raid of revolvers disrupt
summer's inevitable and prodigal retribution.

is the postscript of a furious sweat
allocation of *what'evs* fosters ails—
the Avenue's blunt curves, as elegies
for young boys steadily outnumber strokes
of felt-tip pens on diplomas.

is the prolongation of hands pocketed in excess,

is an addict relinquishing veins to a fraternal sponsor,

is fiber optics siphoning electricity to a vigil house,
where a mother waits for a son
whose heart is somewhere rehearsing
a non-esoteric song called *silencio.*

>weary are the days, gang-cropped and curt—this
>valet of regress, without hesitation fails to object
>to the gray matter's decapitation

when will this be the beginning of the end,
the beget that begets the cell's incessant rendition
of rebirth and reveille,
the day when noses have had enough
of the angel-dust high of evidentiary gunpowder?

at the brim of these lipped hours—
there's more than gators in the swamp
that will kill us

stand your ground
kiss the ground

there's something more bitter
than cold that will puncture our lungs
like bursts from a lipped trumpet:

      a lowly and dour black wallet
      a star-burst mallet

there's something in the spin of our spindle
that is sifting youth like wheat—

it's treason to bury these jejune bodies—
some traditionally, the others above ground

      kiss the ground kiss the ground

rat attack tact tact tact tact

splitting the macho
splitting the macho,
splitting the macho,
splitting the map, *yo!* . . .

why weren't we born to stints of beauty?

      drubbing is a felony—
      why aren't we all cellmates?
      History's not that dumb.

economics of corroded carburetors and stalled
transmission have become a respite
for the gasping—flickers

of headlights where we once made
a trustee out of resilience, made it
habit to forgive stiff joints, now gone

the malice is in the alibis

      we believe, we believe—

the ego lies, as we watch pensions
gallop toward the edge of the city
to be swallowed up in the new edition
of *How the Other Half Lives.*

at the brim of these lipped hours—
      is that unmistakably labored tone
      that separates bait from those who know it;

      that tenement-ed ever after:
      one of the begets that begat the permutation
      of *I before see*
      until it became a new fermentation;

            one of those begets that begat
            walking around with loaded fists in pockets,

            that begat some a whole lot of love
            with nowhere to putt it—*can't aim at*
            a hole when you're living in it—

      is that firmament where the cool blue of lost bodies
      goes *puff puff* all the way gone,

      is that unmistakably labored breath that separates
      bait from those who know

we were born equal
but bred as below average
in cities of land we owned,
land we toiled one hundred
percent and over—very same
places and tenements today:
nurseries, hiding place—some cold-framed with crime

       despair 'til nothing's left but to make bad
       bargains—the young among us—so reads
          testimony
       of causes—all who had lost connection with
          home-
       life or never had one, when traced back
       to the very places—at that early stage of being
       acquired—on those ships: lies lies lies of how
       the other half lived

The most was made of us while it lasted—
took to cities that stirred and grew, that soon
filled cellar to top story, with an evil
more destructive than wars.

at the brim of these lipped hours—
       official reports read:
       the whole land, forlorn and forsaken—
       and you believe these "truths"?

       this, after our necks were kept strung,
       babies kept dizzied, this, after hands
       were kept busy—from sun-up to sun-up.

       The most was made of us while we ghosted.

How could we have known nothing
what would be left was to make bad
bargains or that the cheapest way out
would in time become an evil offspring;
and we, infamous ever after in our ditties?

at the brim of these lipped hours
we believed, we believed these *truths*
to be—

how many of us would make it?
we're told *hundreds of thousands wouldn't* though
millions already footed the bill—
more than a century's drift from where we once
called home—to which we are now too
often strangers—the begat vagrancy
that begat vacancy upon vacancy upon—

History's built
for this
purpose?

We knew how to make a look an omen
but split in level-headedness, in the settling
of scores. In fairness, how could we have known
about evil offspring more destructive
than wars, or being infamous
ever after in cities, earning nothing
more than interest and left to make even
more bad bargains?

at the brim of these lipped hours
                we believed—

                we believed
                these truths
                to be
                self-
                evident

      —most who had been of use
      had been used
      many of whom mistook freedom
      for free, use for living—
      were dragged again, to fields—not
      by force not by choice

still a class of tenants living hand to mouth—History's
built for this purpose. Work went on—

untold
depravities:

      every lie has a sponsor
      though it's clear some of us did dirt
      the history that of many of us drew dirt prematurely is
      stricken from record—a family's famine genealogy

      deficit begat deficit begat deficit—
      begat terms that perpetuate a golden oldie:

      doctor, lawyer, preacher, teacher
      father, mother, still, nigger

this while our necks were kept
strung, babies kept dizzied—

      split that cord for psalm—

History, whose night won't be split
like air on a lipped trumpet?

at the brim of these lipped hours
we're still making a way,
but like John the Baptist, being level-headed gets us
beheaded—*spit that psalm* for palms raised,

for wails that hail a fleeting respite,
for gums split 'til they numb—

History's not dumb
but pathological:
black lives *matter* suppurate
the brown-lipped split, read
as an omen—

leveling all our best, 'cept when to glorify wrists
on the hard-court / speed
on the gridiron / eagle
on the green—just takes one
to spoil the class—

it's the result of forget-
fulness, it is one
of the ways evil has
of avenging itself.

at the brim of these lipped hours—
we dream, we dream
but no one dreams this way:

no one dreams *one day I will quail*
upon a proverbial pavement of red,
and white, and blue

no one dreams that a city of monuments
would be erected upon the unmarked graves
of those who braved being sold apart.

Oh, History!
those who don't learn
from you
                  are doomed
to repeat you   but some
profited from you—

branding demonstratively
their knock-off sonorous rants
as a new anthem; how could we
have known this evil more destructive than wars
would offspring

at the brim of these lipped hours
is the hour of
enter
gray
shun

is the begat that causes one brother to say to another:
>*black women are harder to love*
>*than white women*

this after centuries of harboring love in the marrow
of a bruised spine—a love toiled one hundred percent
and over—moan so long they hone groan
'til that wail out of an offspring's mouth
splits the air like a lipped trumpet

>brothers, fathers gone so long
>they mime life
>this *I gotta go and be somebody*

>the begat that begat the lie:
>*revolution is an absentee ballot*

>the begat that begat the lie of our exile
>*we the balance of grave ships*

the truth is in the marrow of the spine
brothers in the ever after, walking around
with loaded fists in pockets—

splitting the macho
splitting the macho
splitting the macho
splitting the match, yo!

—carrying syphilitic inflictions
all the way back home

how could we have known
this absence would offspring
with not much left but to make bad
bargains?

at the brim of these lipped hours
we split
our tongues
gnashing on a glass healing

from swirling the razor blade of a horrid past
around our mouths, dubbing
we own it

this blade that seeps into the marrow of our mind
lobotomizing with lies

>the begat that begat the anthem
>*there's two types of black people*

>the lie that begat
>>A Free Can Americans
>>Verses
>>An other

braved the road
from split-head
in the morning
to split head
at night

we wailed we wailed we wailed
splitting the air like bursts
from a lipped trumpet

graved the load
of what was left
and parlayed the abomination
into a praise song

> *Obama Obama Obama*
> *Obama Obama Obama*

we wake still?
dag!
split his lid
for leader

we're free but not
care free

still a class gnawing on that ceiling
splitting our songs into a memory

this what we did before hypomnesia

this Pat Booned "we shall overcome"
coming out the mouth of history

splitting the map yo
splitting the map yo
splitting the map yo
splitting the match, yo!

at the brim of these lipped hours
is the barrel of our hue
                    our humiliation

in that *kept kept kept* nation
paraded in our withdrawals
for the whole world to see

flagging the bicameral
"the past is history"

thought we requited that,
that dumb other, long ago

how could we have known that this evil
would offspring
and that we'd be brought back
here not
by force not by choice
with that dumb other that still prowls
in our ears without a trap

or that one day we'd stumble over
something resembling a memory, wedged
in the marrow of our spine
the memoir of our first arrival

or that one day
a snowflake
would invade our throats
and we'd carry its exile
all the way home?

Prelude (rhite wegrets: an american saga)

once was a mammock
on a hango tree

with a sign that read:
        liggers are nazy.

nangling was another:
we noose diggers.

VII.

"It is not easy to be free and bold!
It is not easy to be poised and bound!"
~ Martin Carter

When History Returns as a Four Hundred-Year-Old Scapegoat

My youngest son, at three, tells me *you're welcome* when I tell him
I love him. He's not wrong. It's much easier to love when one has
somebody to love. Love is a muscle so I thanked him for allowing me
to flex it. He is young and one would think he is not able to choose but
he's not wrong. One time, we watched a show together about penguins
and much was made about their ability to mate for life. *They can't fly
away*, I thought, as if freedom is based on the ability to have a choice.

My seven-year-old asks why *firemen used to drown black boys;* why
they aimed their hoses until the young black bodies stopped moving.
This was after watching a short film on Martin Luther King Jr. day—
the film included King's speech and some photos of hydrants over-
flowing with rage toward a crowd, children among them. This was
for school—he was given the *proof* for celebrating King's birthday.
They couldn't get away, he said. *Why would they do that to Blacks?*

The police and their dogs were obvious choices: keep the peace in riot
gear. But there were the firemen and their long hoses & the hospitals—
doctors who swore an oath to break an oath wrapped up in an enigma.
There were pastors & bishops and priests who taught us about a White
savior who offered the other cheek—they left out he also flipped tables.
& how blood poured out from his pores from the threat of persecution.
& how true salvation must be one's choice. This is their sin of omission.

But sometimes, I forget about forgiveness, & how it is a personal choice.
& I forget about atonement until a question is asked that I cannot answer
without first talking about the chains & the trees & the ropes & cameras.
& how history is being rewritten on a ledger made of freshly born flesh.

& sometimes, being Caribbean-born & Black American, I forget it's winter.
Sometimes I forget it is winter, in America. Sometimes I forget it's winter
in America & I'm not welcomed. Sometimes I forget it's winter in America

and I am not welcomed to be the master of my own decisions. Sometimes I
forget it is winter in America & I am not welcomed & choice is an illusion.
Sometimes I forget when it is winter. In America, choice's always an illusion.
And it always comes back to having to answer questions for which my body
is never prepared. My oldest son asks if God is White. He is certain that God
must be White. *Nothing ever happens to White people who do evil things to
Black people in this country*, he says. They always get away with doing evil.

American Emblem (The Saga of a Black Avenger)

In the end, Captain America hands over the shield
to Falcon (Sam), who feels he's not worthy of it. He is
not your uncle Sam, but a dapper black man in a fresh
fade and tight line-up. He's neither comfortable nor is he
certain—even in a make-believe universe where some
marvel & grapple with life in realms & portals—about
what it means to be a Black Captain America; not even
in the aftermath of a world he helped to bring back from
the brink of utter destruction—ash still fresh in his nares.
My youngest son, wrestling with sleep, wears the emblem
of the shield on a T-shirt. He says he doesn't like to sleep
as if he were afraid of an icy seventy-year slumber himself.
At three, he has already embodied a spark of what it means
for a black man to wear a bullseye on his chest—sleeping-
while-black is not make believe. And Sam knows this too
as he stares into the distance between he and the world as
if he's conjuring another word for reverence. The shield's
more allegory than metaphor: when Captain was found in
that frozen wreckage, his glory and shield were fully intact
—which is to say America and all its promises were still his
to behold. Sam knew that, even after his many tours fighting
against all enemies, foreign and domestic, black superheroes
still need to prove they have earned their moment. The shield
is no different. It's the American way: favor ghosts & legacy
over second-comings. *A rebel spirit is upon us,* they'll say, &
preserve Captain's legacy. Sam knows this wrought arithmetic
long held by the empirics, that a four-hundred year revenge
was at hand, so he kept his hands in the custody of his pockets

until, Bucky—Captain's lifelong friend—nods his approval.
He knows what we all know: even in the make-believe world
of Gods & Monsters, a black superhero—Captain's wingman
—still needs a white sponsor to become a true American hero.

American Witness

i wish i could write about bees and collapsed colonies &
about **a young child frolicking through fields of** withered
posies in search of something **whole and tender** and **with**
his head down and crying about the **promise of the unseen.**

i wish **this could be a verse about** extinction and preventing
lions & other wildcats from meeting the fate of a rifle's aim
& about how a broken tooth will always remind **us** of Cecil,
whose murder caused **a nation** to hold its head down and cry.

i wish i were writing about a beached whale or a pack of sea
lions who mistook the **sand for stardust** or heavenly grounds
& how a village of strangers **nursed & ushered** them **back to**
the **sea**—watching, arm-on-shoulder, & head down & crying.

i wish what is written was about **a rare moth** that once made
a dilapidated shack its home, and how it was **spared minutes**
before demolition, and how it was **a man** who built the shack
that **discovered** it, and how **he held** his head down and cried.

instead i am writing in hope that you will care about **my early**
demise, enough to be moved by how often i find myself **on my**
knees & wailing **under a dilapidated sun** and how your head is
often **constantly held down** so you don't have **to watch me die.**

Notes

1. Excerpt from "Episode" from *Big-Eyed Afraid* by Erica Dawson. Copyright © 2007 by Erica Dawson. Used with the permission of The Waywiser Press.

2. The last section of "American asteRISKS (The George Floyd Suite)" is modeled after the poem "Facts about the Moon" by Dorianne Laux.

3. In section II of "Gray's Anatomy (The Freddie Gray Suite)" the classifications of *homicide* in U.S. criminal law is from Wikipedia.com.

4. In section III of "In Defense of My Body's Dissertation" the definition for the word *strata* is from Dictionary.com.

5. The epigraph "Pressed to the wall, dying, but fighting back!" is from the poem "If We Must Die" by Jamaican-American writer Claude McKay, which was first published in the July 1919 issue of *The Liberator* magazine.

6. "American Reprieve (A Here and Not-Here Division)" is modeled after Rita Dove's *Mother Love*, a book of poems written as Crown of Sonnets, with the following lines borrowed from variations of text from *Minnie's Sacrifice*, a novel by Frances Ellen Watkins Harper: *beneath the shadow of a mighty grief; ever and anon; no trace of an outcast blood;* and the following phrase *no-harm sins* borrowed from the play "Poker" written by Zora Neale Hurston.

7. "Elegy for the American Dream" contains the text *the dead, arrayed in time* from the poem "The Chosen Ones" by Pablo Neruda, as translated by Alfred Yankauer.

8. Epigraph by Dr. Christena Cleveland is excerpted from a speech and is used with permission of Dr. Christena Cleveland, a social psychologist, public theologian, activist, and author of *God Is a Black Woman*.

9. "How to Craft an American Scapegoat" contains the text *huddled masses yearning to breathe free and tired-poor,* from the sonnet "The New Colossus" by Emma Lazarus, which is on a bronze plaque on the pedestal of the Statue of Liberty.

10. "American Pathos (What It Means to Love)" is modeled after the poem "Skinned" by Vievee Francis.

11. "American Lexicon (A Taxonomy of Pride)" uses variations of the lyrics from "America the Beautiful", an American patriotic song written by Katharine Lee Bates.

12. "American Libretto (A Letter of Resignation)" makes use of the following texts: *to fight monsters we create monsters,* from the trailer of the major motion picture film *Pacific Rim; our skin is black from the heat of famine,* from Lamentations 5:10 (American Standard Version Bible); *the whole land, forlorn and forsaken,* from *Souls of Black Folks by W.E.B. Du Bois; we believe these truths to be self-evident,* from the Declaration of Independence; and makes reference to *How the Other Half Lives,* a book by photojournalist Jacob Riis that documented deplorable living conditions in New York City slums in the 1880s.

13. "American Emblem (The Saga of a Black Avenger)" refers to characters featured in *Marvel Studios Avengers: Endgame*, a major motion picture film.